REMBRANDT

ABOUT THE AUTHOR

The Dutch art critic Dr. Hans Redeker began a literary and philosophical career, which led him to the plastic arts. He has written books on *Existentialism, The Crisis of the Artist* and *Religious humanism,* contributed to many periodicals and published monographs on modern painters.

HANS REDEKER

Rembrandt

BARNES & NOBLE, INC.

NEW YORK

Publishers · Booksellers · Since 1873

Editor: Anthony Bosman
Translator: Albert J. Fransella
Lay-out: Wim van Stek
Published in the United States in 1965
by Barnes & Noble, Inc., 105 Fifth Avenue, New York 3, N.Y.
© 1965 and printed in Holland by The Ysel Press Ltd. Deventer

Anyone asked to write about Rembrandt within the compass of a small book must feel like a traveller who has to compress into very few pages the story of many years of wandering over an immense continent. A vast, almost endless, continent, fantastic, wild and full of variety, with lush valleys, rocky-edged precipices, volcanoes and inhospitable mountain ranges, burning hot summers contrasting grimly with barren winters; a land which, though already mapped out to the minutest detail, still presents the traveller, with surprises, enigmas and unsuspected vistas at every turn. For Rembrandt, one of Holland's most famous sons and glorious symbol of those affluent years which the Hollanders call their "Golden Age", was not only one of his country's greatest geniuses —indeed many, even in this present day and age, would say the greatest of them all—but he left behind such a complex oeuvre with so many facets, and of such wide scope and so high a degree of excellence that its like can hardly be found.

This is all the more striking when we place him in his own geographical and historical entourage. Painting in the Holland of the seventeenth century was, more than anywhere else, an art of specialists, each of whom kept mainly to his own genre, to the product his clients wanted and therefore had a ready market, in which the artist himself also dealt, even when it was not essential for him to follow another profession alongside his work as a painter. And in this small republican country where the Church, as a result of Protestantism, had ceased to be a patron of the arts, and where there could no longer be question of patronage by either Court or nobility, such a clientele did indeed exist, not of princes or of noble families, but chiefly of merchants, ship-owners and other well-to-do members of the middle-classes.

In this sense we know Frans Hals as the gifted portrait painter of this self-confident class of Hollanders; Jan van Goyen and Jacob van Ruysdael as the painters of these low-lying lands with their high skies and broad waters; Jan Steen as the master of the often symbolical genre-painting, and the dozens of other painters of portrait or still-life, genre or landscape, of town views, horses, cattle or poultry, of ships and the sea. Even Jan Vermeer of Delft was a great man in a fairly limited sphere; a sphere to which the twentieth-century forger, Han van Meegeren, thought he would add a hitherto absent genre, to the confusion of many of the experts of to-day.

But Rembrandt stands out as a non-specialist in a world of specialists, solitary and challenging, a universal artist who pitted himself against the greatest in the world and tolerated no limitations save those he chose of his own free will; who in all those realms raised art in the Holland of his century to the highest of accomplishments, and yet withdrew, like a strange exotic bird, from the national features and constraints; the only painter of Protestant Holland who, in the words of Jakob Rosenberg, "could have figured prominently in an international exhibition of Baroque painting".

On a closer examination of what has survived of his painting oeuvre, portraits dominate as far as numbers are concerned; of over six hundred works, more than a third are portraits. Early in his career, they certainly formed the basis of his renown and prosperity as *the* most admired portrait painter in Amsterdam. Most of the portraits are of individuals—himself, members of his family and other men and women, known and unknown to us—all revealing his deep interest in human beings. The self-portraits, about sixty of them, are of special interest; they constitute a record of self-examination and self-criticism comparable in penetration to the self-portraits of that extraordinary nineteenth-century Dutchman, Vincent van Gogh.

Then there are a number of double portraits, the most famous of which is the so-called "Jewish Bride" (p. 69). The group portraits fall into several classifications. There are two "anatomy lessons": the first one, "The Anatomy Lesson of Dr. Tulp", (pp. 20, 21) was (in 1632) of decisive importance in Rembrandt's career as a portrait-painter; of "The Anatomy Lesson of Dr. Deijman", of 1656, only a central fragment has survived a fire. There is one example of the *schuttersstuk* (the group portrait, traditional in Holland, of a shooting company, or civil guard): the famous picture miscalled "The Night Watch" (pp. 30, 31). There is only one example of the guild picture, "The Syndics of the Drapers' Guild", (pp. 64, 65) generally considered to be Rembrandt's masterpiece.

Then, also unique in its class, there is the magnificent "Family Portrait" (p. 72).

Of the remaining two hundred or so paintings, 160 are Biblical portraits and scenes, Rembrandt's deeply sincere personal contribution to the Protestant art of his country. Then there are a number of classical and mythological paintings (most of them commissioned works), the most famous of which are the "Danaë" (p. 25) and "Aristotle Contemplating the Bust of Homer".

Quite apart from his other series, we can separate as a small group those rare allegorical and historical compositions of Rembrandt; allegorical, such as the enigmatic "Concord of the State" of 1641; historical, such as the splendid canvas painted during his last period, "The Conspiracy of Claudius Civilis" (pp. 66, 67) which he did for the new Town Hall at Amsterdam, soon afterwards cut up and now a mere fragment in the National Museum in Stockholm.

And finally, as far as paintings are concerned, we still have his landscapes, which—with the exception of those of Herman Seghers—no other painter of Holland has ever charged so dramatically and with such a visionary aspect as did Rembrandt in a middle period of his life's work (pp. 29 and 33).

If, because this review must needs be a summary one, the broad terrain of his art seems to have been somewhat roughly outlined, there still remain two dimensions of his creative ability which, both in present-day opinion and in the eyes of his contemporaries, can be considered as at least equally valuable as the oeuvre of Rembrandt the *painter*. These are the 300 or so plates of Rembrandt the *etcher*, and more than 2,000 examples that remain to us of Rembrandt the master of *drawing*.

In Rembrandt's own lifetime, it had not escaped even his greatest critics that—purely by his own efforts and resources—he had established as a free and independent artistic medium what was in his time the still new art of etching as a result of his experiments with his own unsurpassed plates. And, *mutatis mutandis,* as far as a smaller and more select group of connoisseurs and artists is concerned, the same may be said of his drawings. These are his most

7

intimate and direct forms of expression which, apart from their traditionally preparatory and dependent function as detail studies or composition sketches, also possessed an individual significance and value for the artist himself.

It is in this very direction that the revolution in modern art in our own century brought about the great, regenerating break-through towards the direct and the elemental without which the present, considerably increased, appreciation for what the artist Rembrandt in his elementary "shorthand" had achieved could not have been so exceptionally great, so great, in fact, that it could almost overshadow his significance as a painter.

And so Rembrandt appears to us in an intriguing multiplicity of aspects which seem to melt into each other with the vagueness of the contours of his own paintings. To start with, we have Rembrandt the painter, etcher and sketcher in a broad field of motifs: human, Biblical, mythological and landscape. But except for his drawings we find no genre pictures, and only rarely a work without the figure of a human being, not even in what seems a formidable piece of painting of still-life, "The Slaughtered Ox". Then we have Rembrandt the radical, as the "first heretic in the art of painting", as his contemporary, the poet Andries Pels, saw him.

And later on as the painter who (with an intensity not to be found

either in the realism of his own surroundings or in the idealism outside) knew how to make his art the expression of the deepest and most earnest human experiences, whose art "laden with existentiality", appeals to us much more directly, more vehemently and more intimately than any other painter in the centuries of Renaissance and Baroque.

But here we touch inevitably upon the man Rembrandt, the human being and realist, with whom, as Vincent van Gogh said: "It was not a question of beauty, but of truth". And also Rembrandt the obstinate and unyielding, who, against all the objections of his academically-minded contemporaries, considered a picture completed as soon as, in his opinion, the intention of the painter had been fulfilled. In this respect he was the first modern artist. And now Rembrandt the teacher, the religious Rembrandt, the passionately sensual Rembrandt, the enamoured, the proud, and the tormented Rembrandt. And finally, the young Rembrandt up to about 1640, and the Rembrandt of the last years.

Since Rembrandt is so many-sided it is no wonder that in the centuries since his death there have been distorted and oversimplified interpretations of his character and his art. Every age has created its own Rembrandt in its own spiritual image.

Romanticists have constructed the image of a heroic and tragic Rembrandt, a misunderstood genius; in his old age unappreciated, reviled by critics, poverty-stricken and lonely. But this image, based on half-truths, cannot be maintained in the light of the facts. Up to the day of his death, though he was criticised severely by some, Rembrandt was internationally respected and did not lack admirers in Holland. Even the most revolutionary works of his last years found a surprising amount of appreciation and understanding. As for his loneliness, if he did not mingle with socially prominent people, it was because these people no longer interested him; he found common people more interesting and also enjoyed the companionship of a few men of uncommon intellectual and spiritual qualities.

Then there was the image, also popular in the nineteenth century, of Rembrandt as preacher and shepherd of our souls. From this point of view his pictures were regarded as edifying, as important primarily for their narrative content (the Biblical subjects, especially) and their "spiritual" meaning. But to see only moral and spiritual significance in his pictures is to ignore Rembrandt as an artist and to overlook much of his character as a man.

Now we of the twentieth century, with our fondness for removing masks, gilding and haloes, have an understandable reaction against the earlier romantic and moralistic interpretations of Rembrandt, but we should not allow our passion for "debunking" and our other philosophic and artistic tendencies to lead us, in turn, to construct a distorted and one-sided image of Rembrandt. To deny or minimize or ignore the heroic and tragic qualities of Rembrandt and the drama of his personal and artistic struggles would be to falsify the character of a man and artist of uncommon depth and intensity, a thorough-going non-conformist and rebel. And to see in his paintings only abstract qualities of form and colour—to admire in a Biblical scene, for example, only such things as the realistic painting, or the colours, of a helmet or a cloak—would be to overlook what for Rembrandt was an important element of his art: its religious and human significance.

For Rembrandt was not just an artist who loved beauty; he was a man who all his life was a seeker after truth, freedom and godliness. That is how he was regarded by his contemporaries and how he was described by his three earliest biographers: the German Joachim von Sandrart (in 1675), the Italian Filippo Baldinucci (in 1686) and the Dutchman Arnold Houbraken (in 1718).

Rembrandt van Rijn, son of Harmen Gerritszoon van Rijn and of Neeltgen Willemsdochter van Zuytbrouck, was born in Leiden on the 15th July, 1606. The liberation of Protestant Holland, wrested from the Catholic Kings of Spain, was consolidated in his very earliest youth, though the definitive Peace of Munster only took place in 1648. During that period the theological discord which had rent the young Republic for years was also resolved. The prosperity and power of Flanders and of Antwerp, city of Rubens, were finally broken, and this decline brought new blood to the northern Netherlands and to their artists.

From that time onwards nothing stood in the way of the might and prosperity of Holland and her cities. A spirit of great tolerance prevailed, and this attracted learned and noble-minded men from abroad, particularly amongst the Jews and other persecuted persons. In the meantime the citizens of Holland developed into merchants, ship-owners, regents (governors) and patricians of this characteristic generation of self-confident, energetic personalities, who united the God of the Bible and Calvin with a pronounced talent for trading and an expansive spirit of enterprise, which qualities enabled them to appear in their small, but dreaded, ships on the farthest coasts of the world.

It was they, with their new fondness for luxury and elegance (within limits), their regents' palaces and country mansions and their desire for symbols of social prestige and status, who enabled an art to flourish which stood out most sharply against the influences of Italy and the Italianate Flanders of Rubens and Van Dyck. It was not only the subjects that were different, now that the great tradition of religious art had been abandoned and the walls of the churches were as unadorned as the pictures of Saenredam show us; it was also the style, which was the product of altogether different relationships to the world.

The art of painting in seventeenth-century Holland was an art for private rooms, often of modest dimensions—like the whole culture of the country, which was private and intimate, concentrated in the home. It was the shooting companies and the guilds, associations of free citizens, which provided the social basis—the patronage, that is—for the only Dutch painting that could be called monumental; they demanded carefully composed group portraits in which the artist was to do justice to every member's dignity.

Realism in place of idealism, human beings in place of superhuman persons, everyday realities in place of fantasies—that is the essence of the Dutch art of Rembrandt's day. Thus, Dutch landscape painting developed, to become the model to which later centuries would return again and again. The excessively showy Dutch still-lifes of the sixteenth century were raised to an independent genre of pictorial purity. Jocular and comical—sometimes insinuative—realistic scenes flourished. Domestic interiors appeared. Ships and water were popular subjects, and the painters and sketchers of naval battles actually accompanied the warships. The image of Holland as preserved in Dutch paintings became a permanent monument to a self-willed people with strong characters.

All this art seemed to need was the surrounding reality: human beings and their possessions and the land upon which they had placed their stamp. All the same, it should not be forgotten that the most powerful and dignified members of the upper layer in that era showed a clear preference for the pompous splendour of the Flemish baroque. Moreover, many a merchant's home was a veritable museum of international—especially Italian—art. This Holland, which sailed the seven seas, was by no means a closed or isolated domain as regards the arts.

It is not without significance that Leiden was the birthplace of Rembrandt. For in these days Leiden, lying between Amsterdam, Haarlem and The Hague, was among the richest and most important cities of the Republic, with a prosperous textile industry, and since 1575 a centre of learning with a University. As the son of a miller, whose mill stood within the city limits on the Rhine (whence he took his name), Rembrandt belonged to the middle classes, the core of the people of Holland. He had sisters and brothers; the latter remained in Leiden and were employed in milling, baking and shoemaking. For him (the youngest but one) his parents had in mind a more ambitious career. He went through the Latin School in Leiden, and in 1620, when he was fourteen, he was enrolled in the University.

Though some sources say that he passed for a "learned painter", others describe him as somewhat "unerudite" (his library, with the exception of the book of books of his life, the Bible, was sparse in the extreme). The artistic blood that ran in his veins must have been so strong that in the same year he was placed under the tuition of the local painter, Jacob van Swanenburch (1571-1638), with whom he was to remain for three years, and was able to master at least the technical basis for his calling.

From an artist's point of view, the following six months must have been of more decisive significance, for these he passed in the atelier of the Amsterdam painter Pieter Lastman (1583-1633). It was, moreover, his first contact with the city which was later to consider itself indissolubly identified with him; Amsterdam, the lively harbour town and city of merchants, which, during Rembrandt's lifetime, quadrupled in size by its feverish activities and became a metropolis of 200,000 people, with girdles of splendid canals and its new Town Hall at the Dam.

Rembrandt was then 17 years old, and, according to certain sources, must also have worked for some time in the ateliers of Jacob (or Jan) Pijnas in Amsterdam and of Joris van Schooten in Leiden. But this ended his tuition from direct teachers, and now we see him proceeding under his own sail along other canals—gathering together his own art collection—and in contact with great international works, which he assimilated in his own way.

As was the fashion in those days, Van Swanenburch, Pijnas and Lastman had travelled to Italy to refresh themselves at the source of all great and true art, and returned under the influence of the Roman realism of the early part of their century, with Caravaggio as the most dominating painter. But Caravaggism, with its vehement realism, fortified by a keen and dramatic use of the contrast between light and shade which was called into being by an artificial source of light introduced from the side of the picture (either high or low), the 'chiaroscuro' or clear-obscure, was actually brought to Holland by the Utrecht school, the city of the painters Hendrick Terbruggen and Gerard van Honthorst, where it was already flourishing in 1620-1625. It was, in many variants and degrees, more a general integral ingredient in those days, rather than the monopoly of any one school.

When Rembrandt was about 20 years of age, in 1625-26, and first made his appearance as an artist in painting and drawing, he was by no means a rebel, but (despite early visible personal characteristics) rather a faithful follower of the Italian academic and internationally propagated methods, and he inclined both towards Lastman and towards Utrecht. At any rate, at that point he did not seem to be much occupied with what, in later years, was to develop into a specifically Dutch art.

That beginning is symptomatic. Swayed by an international and rather "conventional" interest, he was to become the lonely genius of the art of painting in Holland, yet to be found nowhere save in this low-lying, damp, country of Protestant people.

With quick strides we follow in his track, as far as the more outward occurrences of his life are concerned, and we find him, from 1626 to 1632, his first period as an independent artist, in Leiden, where he shared a studio with a slightly younger friend and fellow-student, Jan Lievens, and worked so closely with him that in some paintings of those years we think we recognise the hand of both painters. They were two hard-working young artists, who neglected their health for the sake of their art and who, showing what was for those days remarkable independence, would not take the time or trouble to make the journey to the Mecca of all painters: Italy.

At any rate, that is how they were described, in 1628, by Constantijn Huygens, Secretary of the Stadholder of Holland, poet, universal scholar and patron of the arts, and one of the first to recognise the talents of Rembrandt (and of Lievens). For that matter, the 22-year-old Rembrandt had already been described by a connoisseur in Utrecht as a young celebrity. It indicates his rapid climb to fame, even outside of Leiden, that in his twenty-fifth year he decided to leave his native city for Amsterdam, with its many patrons of art.

The works of Rembrandt during those years in Leiden with which we are familiar make his quick success understandable, even if they do only form the preparation for his later greatness. In them some elements which remain constant throughout the whole of his oeuvre are not yet complete or are merely on the surface. First there is his chiaroscuro (light and shade), which later on he was to intensify from a generally used pictorial means to the language of a personal expression. But now it already shows itself in one specific aspect, in so far as Rembrandt uses less the effect of a high or low placed artificial light source, than a high *natural* light streaming inwards from high up or from the side, reminding us of

14

the divine light which was the medium of the stained-glass-window artists of the Cathedrals.

Among those constant factors that appeared so early should be added his special fondness for exotic Eastern apparel and rich materials in which he could dress his models or himself in studies and Biblical scenes. In these models we are able repeatedly to recognise his nearest and dearest ones — especially his mother; his father somewhat problematically, his brothers and sisters — and also himself. He paid great attention to the rendering of his own facial expression and sensitivity, even if this latter is a more external study. Later on, too, there remains throughout his work an unusually close tie between the intimate circle of his own home, his love and his friends, and the figures and motifs of both Bible and mythology.

Another factor is that even while very young Rembrandt shows an unusual preference, not for the blossoming beauty of youth, but for graybeards and others who have been marked by life, have acquired wisdom and dignity, and have become real characters. A painting out of his Leiden period such as "Simeon, or the Presentation in the Temple" (p. 19) unites all these factors. It is a favourite theme of his which often recurs, and has an emotional symbolism as his last, unfinished painting.

This is also a feature inherent in Rembrandt; that he identifies himself with certain Biblical figures and motifs, figures which, in their simplicity and vigour, their piety or their afflictions, remain abidingly the embodiment of the Hand of God and the truth of life.

Rembrandt started etching while he was still in Leiden. And it was in Leiden that he found his first pupils — among them, a neighbour, the young boy Gerard Dou, who became a fine painter, admired especially for his night scenes, who under the influence of Rembrandt became the founder of the Leiden school of genre-painting, characterised by minutely detailed realistic pictures.

Attracted by his many commissions, but perhaps even more because of the amount of work he had to devote to his first big commission "The Anatomy Lesson of Dr. Tulp" (pp. 20, 21), Rembrandt established himself permanently in Amsterdam in

1632; the city which he was not to leave any more except for brief excursions through the countryside, until his death in 1669. He first dwelt in the spacious house in the Jodenbreestraat (next to the "Rembrandthuis") belonging to the prominent art dealer Hendrick van Uylenburch, with whom he had already had business dealings in his last years in Leiden, and in whose business he was interested as a shareholder, with other painters. Van Uylenburch, himself a Mennonite, had an extensive clientèle, especially among the Mennonite merchants, and imported among other things Italian works of art by the shipload. Van Uylenburch had also founded a school of painting where children of good families were educated in this notable art, and this initiative does not seem unconnected with the arrival of Rembrandt. In any case, Rembrandt was in an Eldorado for young artists, surrounded with luxury and culture and in contact with the best of international art.

Meanwhile, with his "Anatomy Lesson" as his visiting card, he was able to trump the card of every other painter in Amsterdam. For compared with his predecessors of the art of group portraiture, he shows himself as a revolutionary radical, on the one hand by his painting technique, the light and shadow or chiaroscuro and the spatiality, and on the other hand by the enthralling and arresting element of the action, and the anxious suspense, together with the manner in which the artist involves the viewer of the picture himself in the scene. From that day, his name was made as a portrait-painter, and he was able to command exceptionally high honoraria for his work.

The house of his art dealer was decisive for Rembrandt in another respect; there he met van Uylenburch's niece, Saskia van Uylenburch, the fairly well-to-do young daughter of a deceased Frisian patrician from the North of the country, and, as his only unmarried niece, still a member of the Amsterdam dealer's household. Rembrandt and Saskia became engaged in June 1633, and three days afterwards she celebrated her 21st birthday. A year later, in 1634, they were married in Sint-Anna-Parochie, a small village in Friesland. About 1636 they were living in the Nieuwe Doelenstraat, "the rich neighbourhood". After living there a short time, they removed in 1639 to their permanent home just next door to van Uylenburch, the proud "Rembrandthuis" in the

Jodenbreestraat (still in existence, but now, as a result of structural alterations, barely authentic any more).

Saskia, by reason of his portraits of her (pp. 22, 23 and 26) and the paintings where we are able to recognise her as the model (p. 25), has become the symbol and personification of Rembrandt's first Amsterdam period, just as Hendrickje Stoffels has for a later period. We think we know Saskia, but only through the brush of the artist Rembrandt. And when Hendrickje appears to us as undeniably much nearer, more intimate, and as a person more sympathetic, then it is certainly to some extent due to the fact that in Rembrandt, both as a painter and an individual, a radical change had taken place. Her "image" appears to us to be the reflected image of his "style".

Here are Saskia and Rembrandt, as they look to us in that famous painting in Dresden with wineglass and peacock, a year after their wedding, he, the coarsely hewn, thickset rustic miller's son from Leiden, with the fleshy face and the bulbous nose, with an excess of the joy of life and sensuality, the triumph of luxury, success and riches, a parvenu compared with the Fleming Rubens. She, more reserved and more distinguished, not as beautiful as a picture, but not without charm, and in a pose that in her case seems forced and not altogether natural. That is how we remember them, even though the picture might have a moralising purport. For us, the Rembrandt of Saskia is the successful young world-conquering painter who—apart from Saskia's dowry—has earned rich sums from his commissions, his pupils and from his graphic oeuvre; whose school of painting on the Bloemgracht was filled with the lively bustle of talented young artists such as Ferdinand Bol and Govert Flinck; whose house was filled with treasures, often exotic, curiosities and works of art, carpets, foreign and old garments and other painters' attributes, which, as an obsessed collector, he had acquired for hard cash at auctions, topping everyone else's bids.

We see him as the man, proud and overweening, who by all kinds of manipulations even forced up the price of his own work. But we see him above all else as the artist who, in his profession, accepted the challenge of the great Rubens, and even endeavoured to outdo in daring foreign artists, as in his "Danaë" (p. 25), in his horror-inspiring "Blinding of Samson" (p. 24), his gift to Con-

17

stantijn Huygens, or in the great Biblical paintings, commissioned through the influence of Huygens by the Baroque-loving stadtholder Frederik Hendrik.

These are examples of a Rembrandt which raise the dynamic mobility, the dramatic tensions and contrasts, the sign language of Baroque, together with his light and shade and a deep wealth of colour, to the utmost degree, and are yet different from the works of the great masters of Baroque; stronger in the pictorial expression of human happenings, but with less natural virtuosity, less monumentality, less elegance of style. Rembrandt substitutes for a wealth of monumental exuberance problems touching human relations.

Compared with all Rubens' fleshly feasts of nakedness, Rembrandt's "Danaë" of 1636, in its erotic anticipation of the marvellous arrival in a shower of gold of her lover, the god Jupiter, is so much more sensually painted, so much more tangible in its personal presence (and is still more eloquent when we know it is historically correct to compare it with Titian's "Venus of Urbino"). And in the whole of the horrific Baroque showpiece the "Blinding of Samson", the human factor, even in the figure of Delila, is a specific and never-to-be forgotten element (pp. 24, 25).

What, in fact, do we know about the still young Rembrandt, apart from the work, as a result of which he is only later to bring to development his real and incomparable contribution to the art of painting, apart from the usually untrustworthy information circulating about him? What we think we can distinguish is an unusually passionate, proud and obsessed artist, with an equally unusually keen temperament and a strongly developed sensual character, a man—in his manner of living and as a collector with all the extravagance and lack of restraint that accompanied this monomania—not really suited to be a good "paterfamilias".

But alongside the somewhat Baroque flourish of his painted compositions, and the master-hand of his portraits, we can also discern the intimate painter of the earnestly human and elementary; the master of drawing, and the etcher. There we see the sheets with the evocative and expressively-inspired line, the drawing that the later painter already anticipates, because the drawer Rembrandt (and the etcher) has always been one pace ahead of Rembrandt the painter. And from those self-same years we also

18   *(Continued on page 73)*

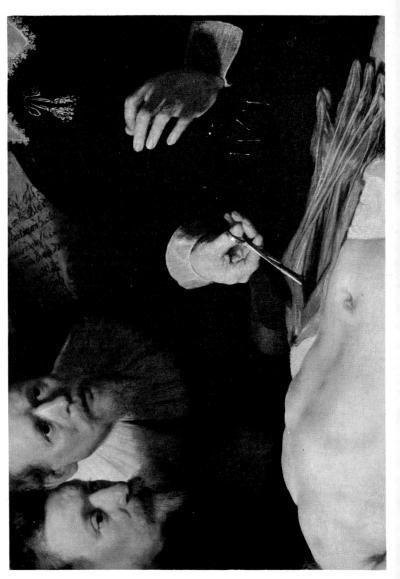

22

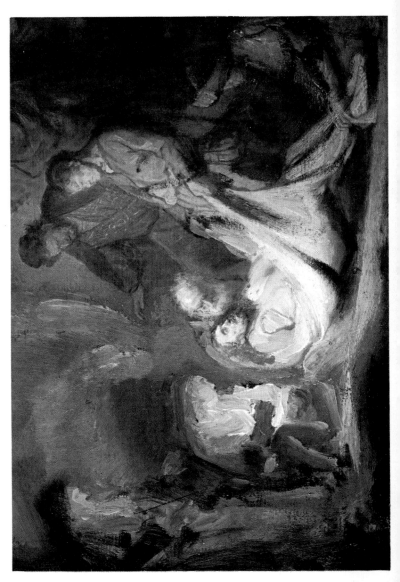

1840.

38

39

40

41

1284. 257

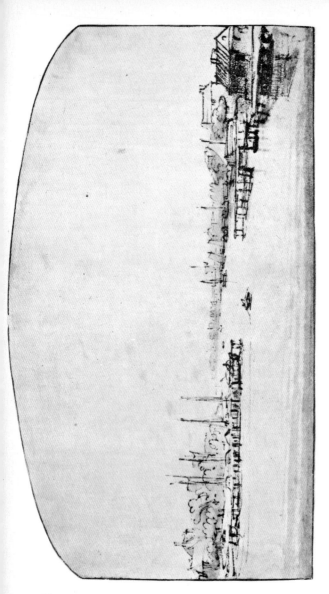

45

51

54

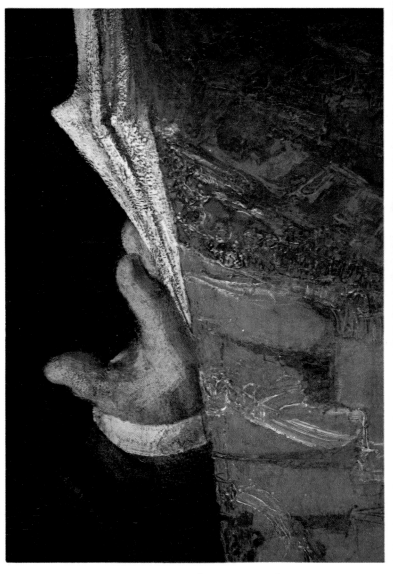

70

72

know that in addition to his many important but often un-interesting patrons and clients he kept close contact with, firstly: the eminent Portuguese Jewish writer Manasseh ben Israel, tutor of Spinoza (and Rembrandt was the first *European* painter of the authentic Jewish individual) and, secondly: with the clergyman Cornelis Claesz Anslo, one of the leaders of the liberal Baptists of the "Waterland" group, called "Mennonites", who, in their Biblical beliefs showed such strong agreement with his own interpretations of the stories in the Bible. Is not our image of the young Rembrandt of the time of Saskia in fact determined by his style?

And what do we know about Saskia? We know her likeness in the first few years, so obviously done by one who loved her; then in intimate domesticity, an artist with his wife (p. 22), and finally a sick woman in bed (p. 26). But was she, with her somewhat bourgeois looks, the woman able to penetrate those deep-lying spheres in which Rembrandt was alone with his problems? Is not our image of her, just as that of Hendrickje, determined by the style in which Rembrandt painted her in his artistry?

The cold facts remain, and they are both sober and sad. Three children, a son and two daughters, all die soon after birth. Saskia herself is sickly by nature, and there seems to have been a probability of tuberculosis in her family, in which many died young. In the new house into which they moved in 1639 they hardly knew any happiness. In September 1641, Titus was born, the only child of theirs who survived, though he too was to die quite early, in his 26th year. Not nine months after his birth, Saskia herself is dead.

All these domestic calamities did not lessen the prolific character of his artistry, and at best heightened the evolution of his art. In the portraits and religious pictures we can already see his style gradually becoming broader and more free, the detail more sober, the use of light and shade more filled with mystery and inner fervour, the spiritual expression less underlined because of the Baroque gestures and movement. We now also see the landscape, with influences of van Elsheimer but chiefly of Hercules Seghers, which penetrate his oeuvre, romantic, dramatic and fantastic, heavily orchestrated as far as the paintings are concerned.

But in his drawings and his etchings, especially in the years before the death of Saskia, we also get to know Rembrandt the walker, who often escaped from his house and the city itself, to discover, just outside the walls, as no other had, the ordinary landscape of Holland, with the waterside, the farms, the windmills and the little cottages, and to note all this with a hand that acquired a steadily increasing freedom and certainty in the recording of all that was most essential (pp. 44, 45 and 48).

In everything that has been painted in this Holland of day-by-day reality and rusticity, there has never been a painter like Rembrandt, who walked the streets of his city and the lanes of his countryside discovering everything with new eyes, recording as it were in shorthand everything that struck him as enthralling in life and landscape, down to the simplest things. By these drawings and etchings the wandering Rembrandt has, as no other, made us familiar with his world, which we are now able to see with his eyes on journeys which we can imagine we are making almost step by step with him.

In the same year that Saskia died (later on he even had to sell her grave because of his debts), Rembrandt completed his greatest commission, which, under the misleading title of the "Night Watch", (pp. 30, 31) was to become, for the entire world, a concept only to be compared with the "Mona Lisa" of da Vinci. It is the processional parade of the Shooting Company, under the leadership of Captain Frans Banningh Cocq, Lord of Purmerland. In another way it is the termination of a period; the unsurpassed summing-up of all the methods he had so far developed from the rudiments of the Baroque, but in a subject typical of Holland. The Shooting Company piece, as a result, underwent a unique transformation.

For what did not go any further in the work of Frans Hals, the great master of the Shooting Company pieces, than a festive and merry party of colourfully decked-out citizens, became in the hands of Rembrandt a mysterious vision which rose far above the occasion, and even to-day still tempts us to speculate about a deeper, historical symbolism. Rembrandt achieved this purely by means of his chiaroscuro (no night, but sunlight gleaming like gold), by the radiant splendour of his colours, by his consummate composition, by his freedom regarding Dutch tradition; above all by seeking for an event, a moment in the midst of daily life, with inquisitive children and a little dog, in which a corporal's section of the Shooting Company move off under command of Captain Banningh Cocq and his Lieutenant Willem van Ruytenburch, a unity of operation in a performance of extreme richness of contrasting action and mobility.

In this genre it has always remained a solitary and unique achievement. It was admired by those surrounding Rembrandt, and received and accepted by the Shooting Company, with entire satisfaction, in spite of the legend of non-appreciation. Neither Saskia nor the "Night Watch" is able to explain the fairly quick alteration in Rembrandt's work of those years.

Just as Saskia in the first period in Amsterdam became a symbol, so has Hendrickje in the second one, until she died six years before Rembrandt. But since recent publications, notably that of Mr. H. F. Wijnman, another woman has appeared who comes between them, a certain Geertge Dircks, the young widow of a trumpeter. She was taken by Rembrandt into his house about a year after Saskia's burial to look after little Titus. For the keenly living and passionate Rembrandt, this became the commencement of a new love affair, which was broken off in 1649, under painful circumstances, when another, younger domestic appeared in his home, and in Rembrandt's heart a new love; she was Hendrickje Stoffels.

We know now that Hendrickje, the farmer's daughter, came from the little town of Bredevoort, and not from Ransdorp, and that the girl who was actually born in Ransdorp in that region above Amsterdam was Geertge Dircks (who so far had been mentioned only in a short and derogatory manner in the literature about Rembrandt). We realize that it was Geertge who got the opportunity of figuring as Rembrandt's model for a number of pictures painted about 1645, who we originally thought was the softer Hendrickje. According to Houbraken: "small of person but well-formed of figure and plump of body", Geertge looks at us with her spirited round face in two studies of a young girl in the costume of North Holland, or as the girl in front of the halfopened door in Chicago, and we can also see her as the "Mary" of the "Holy Family" in Leningrad (p. 35).

We know little else about the role Geertge played in Rembrandt's life, save that she was his paramour and he was enamoured of her. So much so, in fact, that he made her a present of Saskia's ring and her other costly jewels and ornaments. It is because of these riches that we are able to learn more about the end of the story. Her departure in 1649 after violent scenes of jealousy and quarrelling started unpalatable proceedings, a law-suit against Rembrandt on the grounds of broken promises of marriage (probably only lost by her owing to her lower social standing), and an endless re-opening of old sores about maintenance and testamentary conditions in regard to the ornaments.

When she had lost the day, Geertge sought consolation in the dissolute life of Amsterdam, which gave Rembrandt the opportunity, through what were by no means impeccable manoeuvres, to have her shut up as a prostitute in a house of correction. When she became ill her family obtained her release in 1655, and in the following year she died.

In itself, this revealing new chapter strengthened the human side of the image of the painter, whom we consider, not only from the known facts about his life but also from his works, as a warmblooded, passionate and sensual man, who lived his life to the full, was able to love greatly and to hate greatly, and who also, particularly in his passionateness and problem of strong inner conflicts, possessed a sounding board for the language of the Bible, for the stories of sin, suffering and affliction, for love and hate, heavenly mercy and human paltriness.

To pursue the story of his life, this is further dominated by the three factors of love, financial worry and death. The love is, without any doubt, Hendrickje, who was more than "his staunch housewife", and probably his great love, if we are to believe his brush and his pen. She presented him with a daughter, Cornelia, in 1654. The money troubles form—even without exaggerated dramatizing —a really oppressive and endless narrative, for from a time shortly after the death of Saskia, he was faced with pressing liabilities, partially from his house, which he had not yet paid for, partially from the diminution of commissions, and partly from his own nature.

For Rembrandt could not manage money, as Saskia's family had probably already noticed, though in those years it did not seem to matter. But when commissions and pupils both became scarcer, because the artistic course of Rembrandt and the fashion followed by his pupils ran in opposite directions—this occurred in the forties—his difficulties piled up, and his old debts had to be amortized by new ones. This ended by his bankruptcy and the sale of his house, his goods and chattels, in 1657 and 1658, also of his celebrated collection, which we know from the auction sale.

In 1660 Hendrickje and Titus between them formed a company to deal in works of art, with Rembrandt as employee in exchange for board and lodging. This was of course an artifice, not only to save him from further financial worries, but also—in spite of a new bye-law of the Guild of Painters in Amsterdam—to make it possible for him to continue to exercise his profession in Amsterdam. In the same year they were already living in the modest house on the Rozengracht in the Jordaan, a poorer district. From then on, they had to live a very frugal life, in spite of important commissions, such as "The Syndics" and "Claudius Civilis", with admirers from afar and purchasers such as the Sicilian Collector Ruffo, and Cosimo de Medici. A prematurely old painter withdraws from the world into his work. And within that work itself, the figures which now appear (he no longer paints any landscapes) often have the appearance of enigmatic visions, living in their own different reality.

The last facts are in the shadow of death. In 1663 Hendrickje died, never actually married to Rembrandt because of the conditions of Saskia's will. Titus followed her in 1668, six months after his marriage to Magdalena van Loo. When, a year later, Rembrandt died in the house on the Rozengracht, only the little Cornelia was left, with, somewhere in the City, the baby of Magdalena, born after the death of Titus.

What we have gathered from scanty sources, but is confirmed by all his work, is that Rembrandt of those last and great years was a man marked by life, who had laid aside all his youthful vanities and aspirations, and had plunged ever deeper into himself and his work, with no other desire than to be as authentic and as purist as possible and therefore not prepared to make any concessions, even less than in his successful years. Now he is more than ever the man who does not seek the company of men of consequence and riches, but prefers the lower orders, for which he is reproached, and also men of great force of character with wisdom or faith such as the

Jews from Poland, Spain and Portugal. We see a man averse to externals, even as far as his dress is concerned, and with few demands in life. An indomitable individual, indifferent to the conventions, rank or states, and not to be disturbed by anyone in his work. And to these conventions belonged also the laws according to which one was expected to paint.

We see a solitary figure, a non-conformist, but also a man in torment, with a dramatic, stormy soul-life, through the intensity of life and experience, not so much from outside factors, which he had rather called upon himself, but from suffering within. A man with the warmth, fervour and passion which radiate from his last works, with the agitated, vehement, even wild mood which guided his hand in those days. A man of gloom, but who, just because of this, was able to become the painter of the heavenly light of light-and-shade. A keen living, virile man, who, because of that, was able to approach the Bible as the book of books.

In brief, we see a man in the most complete sense of the word, but one who at the same time possessed in a unique way the power to transpose this lonely existence of a keen, passionate, man towards his Biblical God, his struggles within himself and also his moments of mercy and the simple consolation of inner union between man and man into a plastic art of great directness and of revolutionary freedom.

That image of the ultimate and unique Rembrandt as a human being has grown parallel with his evolution as a painter, etcher and a master of drawing until the paintings of the last ten years of his life, in which he stood so completely outside his surroundings and even alone within the western art of painting. It is a development which came gradually to fruition with increasing rapidity during the years 1640 up to about 1660, through all his media of techniques, and elements of language. First as a conquest of all these media in their full richness, then as a sobering and appeasing act, after which, finally, everything that was superfluous, external and traditional, was eradicated, to ensure a final fusion of inner significance, soberness of form and composition, expression of the manner of painting, warm orchestration of colour and the surface pigment, an art going beyond all laws and bounds.

His method of painting was therefore still that of an artist who took every care to produce an exhaustive detailing and expression of the subject matter (p. 21), in order—especially under the influence of the licence to which he is entitled as a master of drawing (and drawing from nature belongs also to his fundamental principles as a teacher)—in the forties—to become steadily broader in order to attain those grandiose brush-strokes and sweeps of colour which he presents to us in a portrait such as that of the young patrician, poet and friend, Jan Six painted in 1654 (p. 57), or the one of Hendrickje of 1658 (p. 60) painted in all its simplicity and earnest, but above all so beautifully painted.

That development continued apace when Rembrandt in his last period broke every thread connecting him with a traditional style of art and, painting with complete freedom and savage violence, scratching, smearing and constructing—with paint brush, palette knife, with the other end of his brushes and even with his fingers—he built up his pictures until at last, out of all this struggle, of which the traces remain in the surface of the pigment, he has created a warm carpet of colour of the most utter opulence.

Here Rembrandt shows himself to be the first rebel of his day, an artist in applying a treatment in which not only the colour but also the touch and the handwriting show themselves as a direct radiation of personal life, inspiration and the rhythm of living, all of which speak their own language; a "botcher" according to his critics—a modern artist in our own century. And yet, in that same period of years, actually in 1661, Rembrandt had demonstrated, with "The Syndics", that he was fully capable of painting the Guild piece, the official traditional group portrait of Holland, with a "restrained elan" and an extreme control of means, and thus producing a masterpiece never to be excelled. This picture, apart from all its other pictorial qualities, is the masterpiece of Rembrandt's genius; the onlooker meeting and seemingly surprising these important gentlemen of the Cloth Guild, and becoming involved personally in the event (pp. 64, 65).

This development of the use of the paint brush to an expressive medium into which the grandiose trend of his art of painting ultimately led, is of course of its very nature inseparable from the other components such as chiaroscuro. For even this play of light and shade, to which he remained true his whole life long, for the whole world the specific "hallmark of Rembrandt", develops along parallel lines, until all external effects disappear, until as a separate artifice it fuses with colour, form, spatiality, into one whole, until it all becomes the bearer of an inner significance.

With this "light in dark" he also creates his own spatiality, no longer definable geometrically, though the finite-worldly and the infinite-heavenly become merged, until an area of light is created in which, with the light, the mystery shines through. In this Rembrandt differs from Carravaggio and the Caravaggists in that he did not use an artificial source of light, placed either high or low, but from the very beginning a diffused daylight, a golden glimmer with somewhat unsharp contrasts, an inter-penetration of light and dark, in which the dark also has its share.

Rembrandt's nocturne, to which the "Night Watch" owes its erroneous name, seem to us therefore to symbolize this earthly existence, the light as mystery, heavenly mercy, a transparent baring of the essential, or in such a dramatic struggle between the forces of light and darkness as in the visionary last state of the great etching "The Three Crosses" of 1653 (pp. 46, 47). But in the last phase it seems that the light no longer shines from a separate source, but from the event itself, and the picture seems to radiate an uplifting warmth from within to the outside, which, with the emotive quality of his painting style and the deep luxuriance of his coloration, combines to make a synthesis of components that are hardly formally distinguishable any longer.

For as far as colour is concerned, we see Rembrandt as the artist who, in ever greater measure, knows how to blend his colorism with his light and shade. If in his Leiden period his pale and cool palette did contain more grey than brown backgrounds, in the Amsterdam period after 1640 these cool and neutral colours receded in favour of deep reds, golden browns and light golds. Red and gold became Rembrandt's favourite diphthongs of colour, together with black and white. As far as pure coloration is concerned, Rembrandt in his last years utilized colour wholly for his own warm luxuriance and his mode of expression, together with his wealth of composition, the emotive, broad and dramatic style of his painting, the fury of the painter, who only seems anxious to give as rich a form as possible to his emotions and to what is possessing him. That is the horrible aspect of his "Conspiracy of Claudius Civilis", an historical theme from the struggle between the Romans and the Batavians, commissioned for the new Town

Hall on the Dam, but rejected (pp. 66, 67). That also blossomed as a unit of human affection and pictorial abundance in the "Bridal Pair" about 1665, which has been baptized as the "Jewish Bride", in which it is immaterial whether we are dealing with Biblical figures or real portraits (p. 69), and in the still later "Family Portrait" in Brunswick (p. 72).

But with Rembrandt as well, colour, light and style serve a form, which is directed to rendering and communication. And that form is the commencement, as far as composition and effect is concerned, and does not differ from the traditional method taken over from Italy; an abstract composition outline which is then filled in and built up from carefully studied details, just as one can differentiate in the preliminary studies between composition sketches and detail studies. In the period which closed with the "Night Watch", the rudiments of the Baroque come to the front; external movements, strong accents and contrasts, exalted expressions of character and mood, and dynamic composition. But after 1640 a change took place here too. The compositions became more restful and simpler, not directed to the element of external mobility but on inner significance, the occurrence evoked as in a stilled moment with all pictorial means of atmosphere, light, spatiality and colour, and the human being who, by an attitude, a hand, a gesture, can express the unspeakable and make the invisible visible. And there, where there is no more action, the miracle takes place. It is the Biblical scenes painted, etched or drawn, which show us in the clearest fashion this penetration to visibility of the inner significance in silence, especially where Rembrandt reverts through the years to certain motifs. Here also we seem to recognize the strong kinship between Rembrandt and the Mennonites, with whom he mixed socially. This small sect outside the great religious denominations rejected all dogmas, sacraments, or interference by state or church, and wished to live in sobriety, uprightness and humility, in the evangelical simplicity of the poor in spirit, and for them baptism had to be a personal decision in later life. They were pre-eminently a group of people who lived according to the Bible, and for whom every story in it had its own meaning, and its own indications for their personal life.

It was those stories and those figures which the Master Storyteller Rembrandt put together with pen or brush. No mass scenes, no heaven, no hell, no creation or apocalypse, but the simplicity of "Tobit and Hannah" (p. 68), the intimacy of "The Holy Family" (pp. 35 and 49), the miracle of Christ, "Christ appearing as a gardener to Mary Magdalene" (p. 50), "The Sacrifice of Abraham" "Saul and David", "Esther", "Jacob and Esu", "Susannah and the Elders" (p. 36), "The Prodigal Son", "The Denial of St. Peter", "Simeon", "Anna", and the "Presentation in the Temple".

With an ever-stronger accent on Christ and the Passion, Rembrandt—in spite of the many Italian, German or Flemish examples —has found expression for all these motifs as a completely unique and personal creation. The Protestant and Biblical art of Rembrandt has in any case only an incidental and indirect connection with the whole European tradition of ecclesiastical art and iconography. It became, especially in later years, in drawings that have an independent meaning and are not meant as preliminary studies, a completely intimate and personal art of avowal, a signed monologue.

When Rembrandt appears to us in a self-portrait during one of the most difficult periods of his life as St. Paul; when in the "Jewish Bride" we hesitate between portrait and Biblical theme, and when, besides his self-portrait as St. Paul, we see several more Apostles, who at the same time could be mysterious fellow-citizens, then this is only the expressing of the fact that the Biblical and the personal in the art of Rembrandt have become fused into an intimate personal human life.

Rembrandt's greatness is only partially revealed in his paintings, and then chiefly in those of his last period. Even if nothing more had been known of his oeuvre than his drawings, his etchings, or of both of them together, then his place of honour as an artist would have been just as high. In both forms of art, as a pioneer, and solely by his own efforts, his originality and his genius, he has brought a fresh medium in pictorial art to the highest summit of evocative strength.

In the case of etching, this was a new technique of graphic multiplication, applied first in the sixteenth century by German graphic artists, further developed mainly by the French artist Callot, but after him explored for the first time in its own, autonomous, possibilities by Rembrandt and also in part by

Hercules Seghers. The case of drawing, on the other hand, was a question of an art medium of very short standing; as far as drawings as definitive and valid works of art are concerned, these were made for the first time a century earlier than Rembrandt in the Germany of Albrecht Dürer, using a technique that is not only cheaper, but is more direct, quicker, more sensitive and more intimate.

In the case of Rembrandt especially, drawing was such a central, determining and fundamental element of his pictorial creative ability that one cannot eliminate it from the pages that have been written about our artist. In point of fact, this must of necessity also be a book about the draughtsman Rembrandt, however summarily this separate chapter has to be gathered together. And in this case too it is a story of development which runs far ahead of the evolution of his painting, but shows a similar growth towards mastery, which is towards an ever-stronger evocation and expression, with a constantly greater economy of means, in a "shorthand" that works wonders with just a few lines and a sweep or two. That development began chiefly in red and white chalk which, with respect to Utrecht, would point above all to Italy as the source of the chalk. But when the chalk later became more scarce its role was taken over by pen, pencil or ink which became the means, by way of pen-and-wash drawings, whereby Rembrandt was enabled to make his notes with a constantly more sure, quicker and more sensitive hand for himself or for friends and pupils, but not as a commercial article.

He drew whatever he saw; the people in the street, every-day things, the reality of his own private life; the houses of his City; the wide waters of the Amstel and the river IJ and everything that he discovered beyond. He drew the motifs of the Old and New Testaments in their intimate humanity; he drew the nudes of Hendrickje and other models with a sensuality changed into piety through love, an imperfection washed clean by love (pp. 39, 40.). He drew life in daily simple reality, caught in thousands of fleeting moments, until—by seeing with the hand of the draughts-man—he could revolutionize the entire old academic tradition with thumb-nail sketches, which have nothing to do with settled proportions or definitions of spatiality, with modelling or pers-pective, which do not even have to keep to the contours, but which—as with no other evocative medium—work and are charged with inspiration, with passion and with life, which seem to have an electrifying effect from stroke to stroke. And when, later on, he uses the reed pen, this gives a powerful stroke which one can blend with a whole variety of tone qualities to extract a maximum of expressive and sensitive possibilities from the linear outline of the drawing. In this way his drawings became an unsurpassed field of creativeness, of incessant renewal, of an inexhaustible story-telling, but in the elementary directness and simplicity of a "token", of a diary, an intimate book of account and confession, but in the language of penmanship, in the forms he had discovered around him with fresh eyes, in the symbolism of one who lived with the Bible.

Broadly speaking, this also holds good for Rembrandt the etcher, who had first to begin to free etching from everything which, in its application, was reminiscent of the older technique of engraving, in order to utilize its possibilities as fully as possible; as the direct, quick, freely noting and sensitive vehicle; sensitive both in the possibilities of line and of the mordant tone. And just as Seghers did, Rembrandt progresses, especially in later periods, with etching and engraving with the burin to combine what, after using the etching needle, was incised by the acids and what, after using the dry-point, remains on the etching needle as a burr, in order to give a still broader field of expression to the line.

In this manner a unique oeuvre was created, which remained famous all his life, in which all his motifs and specific characteristics are repeated, but now expressed in a medium which lent itself just as well to the most elementary lineation as to the most velvety of blacks in tone, and of an extremely heightened play of hatching lines, to all shades of grey, of transparent twilight, and of light and shade. And here as well, restlessly experimenting and constantly seeking, we see Rembrandt taking the same plate (at times an old one, or one belonging to someone else) and working on it for new effects, new solutions, improvements, conceptions and ideas, so that we know of many superior states that in some cases could lead to completely new works of art. Drawing on the etching plate, inking it, printing it, removing it, and constantly bringing it back again, had become a fascinating and almost magical happening for Rembrandt. In this way, during his most

Baroque period, he worked up to a velvety, pictorial, fluent richness, to revert again, particularly in his later work, more strongly to the line and the genuinely graphical. The unparallelled example of this is "The Three Crosses" (pp. 46, 47) where, in a scene of terror, grief and bewilderment almost impossible to describe, the whole of this central historical occurrence is delineated in lines of light and night; both doom and mercy are depicted by the art of etching, as the visionary expression of line.

With all his genius, and as far as such eloquent abstract qualities of his work are concerned, Rembrandt in the end surely remains the painter, the etcher and the drawer of the human being, even though he had to pass through the Baroque and grapple with virtuosity to do so. Moreover, he is not a virtuoso in the sense of a Tintoretto, a Rubens or a Frans Hals, but rather a plodding, laboriously wrestling seeker, a re-builder out of discord, a stubborn and troublesome rebel, a hard-pressed man, but a painter obsessed with an ideal. For us he is above all a painter of human beings, because he liberated them from Italian idealizing, and delivered them from the bourgeois externals of Holland. Because, as an artist, he came into their homes in his unembellished simplicity, his intimacy, his warmth, his dignity, and in what for him were the bare essentials for existence.

That is what his academic critics, his censuring, petty critics, reproached him with, that he didn't paint beautiful goddesses but ugly servant girls. Or servant girls as goddesses, for Hendrickje as Flora is perhaps the most sorrowful goddess in the whole history of painting. And that, in conclusion, he only consorted with inferior people and those of noble spirit. And that he bartered the ideal of the beautiful for that of the voice of truth.

But when Rembrandt pictured the ugly reality as it really was, and added to it a proud indifference for the laws of anatomy, perspective and all, and appeared to bewilder them, he did know how to clothe that ordinary man with a greater dignity than all the goddesses of his competitors possessed. And when he, in the fifties, drew or painted nudes, who were all still redolent of the bed, and bore all the indications of this earthly and harsh existence, as though they came out of the novels of Simenon, they are not to exchanged for any Venus (pp. 38, 39).

There is more real religion in one of the nudes of the sensual Rembrandt than in all the painted angels of Italy. He shows us the human being, not merely as an object, but by means of the sum total of his gifts as an artist, and his own participation in it events in life, he portrays his fellow man in an atmosphere of piety and love. That is why portrait and Biblical or mythological figures, coinciding in space and time, unnoticeably merge together. And this, in a concentrated form, returns to us once more in his self-portraits, where he is no longer (as he was at first) exterior material for study, but where the portraits converse with and confront the beholder. Where they talk, until the last twilight, about the double nature of the human being: the actor and the observer, the one masks himself for the role he is playing, just as the other shows himself without his mask. They are not only tragic or ironic, the roles he plays as an old man, nor only an old man in defenceless self-revelation. They are both: an old man who, in his roles, can also see through his disguises, and lets us know this in his painting (pp. 70, 71). And now there is hardly any distance remaining from what he almost simultaneously painted towards the end of his life: a Return of the Prodigal Son, and a Simeon in the Temple.

LIST OF ILLUSTRATIONS

On pages 8 and 9 portraits (etchings) of Rembrandt, his mother and father, about 1630-31